THE WEIRD AND WONDERFUL WORLD OF BUGS

A BOOK ABOUT BEETLES, BUTTERFLIES, AND OTHER FASCINATING INSECTS

REA MANDERINO, PhD

ROCKRIDGE
PRESS

Interior and Cover Designer: Regina Stadnik
Art Producer: Tom Hood
Editor: Sabrina Young
Production Editor: Jenna Dutton

Photography James H Robinson/Science Source, cover and pp 4, 36, 37, 43; iStock, cover and pp 5, 19, 22, 29, 42, 44; Antony Cooper/Alamy, pp i, 23; SPL/Science Source, pp 2, 27, 31, 33; Steven Valinski/Alamy, p. 3; Nature Picture Library/Alamy, p. 3; John Mitchell/Science Source, p. 4; Scott Camazine/Alamy, pp 6, 16; David M Phillips/Science Source, p. 7; Rick & Nora Bowers/Alamy, pp 8, 21; Science Photo Library/Alamy, p. 8; Millard H. Sharp/Science Source, p. 9; Brian Lasenby/Alamy, p. 9; Cindy Sutton/Alamy, p. 10; blickwinkel/Alamy, pp 10, 26, 45; Gary Meszaros/Science Source, pp 11, 32; Danita Delimont/Alamy, p. 11; Jason Ondreicka/Alamy, p. 11; Dennis Flaherty/Science Source, p. 11; iStock, p. 12; Christopher Price/Alamy, p. 13; Ekaterina Hill/Alamy, p. 13; Henri Koskinen/Alamy, p. 14; Ivan Kuzmin/Science Source, p. 15; Bryan Reynolds/Alamy, pp 16, 43; Jean Landry/Alamy, p. 17; Gerry Bishop/Alamy, pp 17, 23; Skip Moody/Dembinsky Photo Associates/Alamy, pp 17, 41; John Serrao/Science Source, p. 17; Shutterstock, p. 18; Marcos Veiga/Alamy, p. 19; NHPA/Science Source, pp 20, 34; Gustavo Mazzarollo/Alamy, p. 21; Jane Howard/Science Source, p. 22; Andia/Alamy, p. 24; Frank Lane Pict/Science Source, p. 25; Dinodia Photos/Alamy, p. 26; Valerie Giles/Science Source, p. 27; PureStock/Alamy, p. 27; Spirit Otter/Alamy, p. 27; Arto Hakola/Alamy, p. 28; Michal Fuglevic/Alamy, p. 29; L.A. Faille/Alamy, p. 30; Daniel Borzynski/Alamy, p. 31; Ivan Kuzmin/Science Source, p. 32; Rod Planck/Science Source, p. 32; Dante Fenolio/Science Source, p. 35; Buddy Mays/Alamy, p. 38; Nigel Cattlin/Alamy, p. 39; Michael Stubblefield/Alamy, p. 40; Dalius Baranauskas/alamy, p. 44; Author Photo courtesy Steven Waner.

ISBN: Print   978-1-64739-732-6
       eBook 978-1-64739-434-9
       R0

What are Bugs?

Earth is home to more than one million different bugs. They have lived here for more than 550 million years—longer than flowers, frogs, and even the dinosaurs!

Bugs are **ARTHROPODS**. Arthropods have a hard skin called an **EXOSKELETON**. They must shed this skin in order to grow. Arthropods also have jointed legs, which means their legs bend in several

places. The animals we call bugs include **INSECTS** (a bug with six legs) and **ARACHNIDS** (a bug with eight legs). Let's talk about insects first.

All insects have three body parts: a head, a chest, and a belly.

HEAD   THORAX   ABDOMEN

EUROPEAN HONEY BEE

An insect's head has eyes, a mouth, and antennae. They use their antennae to smell. Adult bugs have one to three little eyes called **OCELLI**. Ocelli can only see light. Insects also have two bigger **COMPOUND EYES**. Each of these eyes is really hundreds of tiny eyes that work together. Insects have all kinds of mouthparts. Chewing mouths are called mandibles. Others have mouths like straws that suck up liquids. There are many more!

The chest is called the **THORAX**. The insect's legs and wings are connected to its thorax. Most insects have four wings, but some have only two. Insects can use wings to fly or for protection.

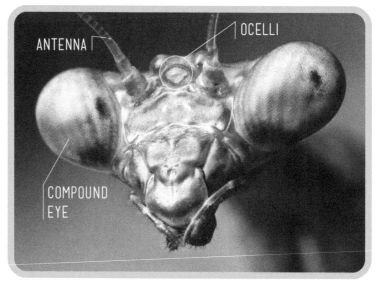

CAROLINA MANTIS

Some insects use their wings to make sounds. Not all bugs with wings fly, and some bugs have no wings at all!

The belly is called the **ABDOMEN**. This is where you will find the bug's guts and fat. On the sides of the abdomen and thorax are little holes. These holes are called **SPIRACLES**. The insect breathes through its spiracles.

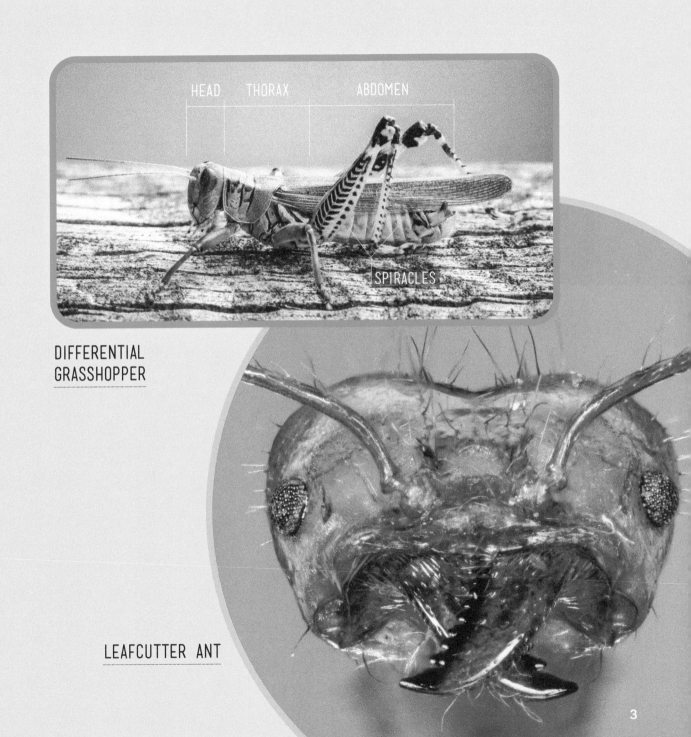

HEAD   THORAX   ABDOMEN

SPIRACLES

DIFFERENTIAL
GRASSHOPPER

LEAFCUTTER ANT

3

MAGICAL METAMORPHOSIS

Insect bodies change in stages as they grow. This is called **METAMORPHOSIS**. Most insect babies hatch from eggs. Then they begin the Eating Stage. They shed their skin as they get bigger.

The last time they shed their skin, their fully developed wings appear. They enter the Flying Stage! This is when insects fly, look for mates, and lay eggs.

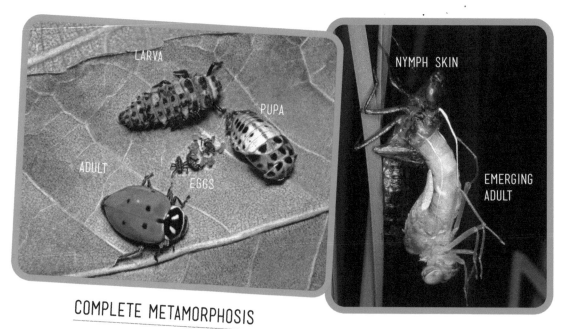

COMPLETE METAMORPHOSIS

INCOMPLETE METAMORPHOSIS

Some insects look like their parents when they hatch, but without wings. These babies are called **NYMPHS**. These insects go through incomplete metamorphosis. Nymphs eat the same type of food as their parents.

Some insects don't look like their parents when they hatch. These babies are called **LARVAE**.

Larvae eat different food than their parents. When larvae are done eating, they shed their skin and start the Sleeping Stage. Insects in the Sleeping Stage are called **PUPAE**. Pupae are growing, but they cannot see, eat, or move much. After a pupa sheds its skin, it has wings and legs. These insects go through complete metamorphosis.

HOW BIG IS THAT BUG?

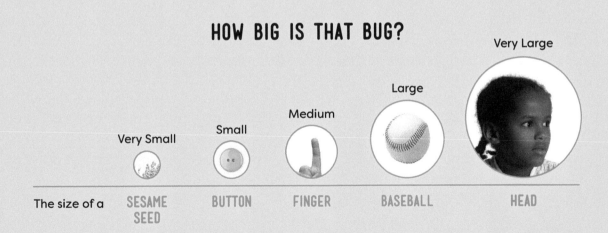

The size of a	SESAME SEED	BUTTON	FINGER	BASEBALL	HEAD
	Very Small	Small	Medium	Large	Very Large

magnificent moths

Moths are insects with big, patterned wings. Their wings have tiny scales on them, like shingles on the roof of a house.

Many moths are brown or yellow to blend in with tree bark and leaves. Brightly colored moths may have poison in their bodies. Birds that eat the poisonous moths get sick. They quickly learn that bright colors mean "don't eat me." Moths often hold their wings around their bodies like a cape when resting.

A moth mouth is shaped like a coiled tube. This is called a **PROBOSCIS**. It uncurls to sip nectar from flowers.

PANDORUS SPHINX MOTH

Many moths drink from flowers at night. Some moths don't drink at all. Moth antennae can look like feathers or thin stalks.

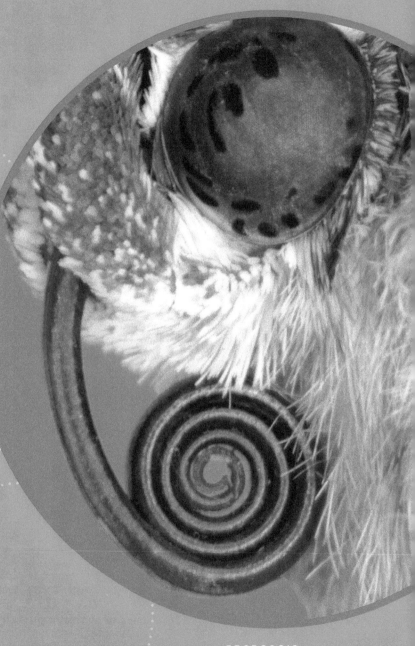

SCIENTIFIC GROUP:
Lepidoptera

SIZE: Very small to large

FOOD:
Larvae: Plants and leaves (on trees or crops)
Adults: Nectar from flowers (some adult moths don't eat)

HOME: Forests, meadows, prairies, deserts, swamps, and fields

METAMORPHOSIS: Complete

Moths usually fly at night and look at the Moon to figure out where they are going. If they see electric lights, moths get con-fused and fly to the lights instead.

PROBOSCIS

Beautiful Butterflies

Butterflies are special moths that **EVOLVED**, or changed over time, to fly during the daytime. You probably see many more butterflies than other moths because they are awake when you are!

When they are not flying, butterflies hold their wings together like a closed book. Their antennae are long and thin. The tips may be round or hooked. Butterflies use their proboscises to drink from flowers during the day.

Butterflies have six legs, but some look like they only have four! Their front legs are tucked close to their bodies and can be hard to see.

BRONZE COPPER BUTTERFLY

PAINTED LADY BUTTERFLY

SCIENTIFIC GROUP: Lepidoptera

SIZE: Small to large

FOOD:
Larvae: Plant leaves, stems
Adults: Nectar from flowers

HOME: Forests, meadows, prairies, deserts, swamps, and fields

METAMORPHOSIS: Complete

ZEBRA SWALLOWTAIL BUTTERFLY

THE WING SCALES
OF A MONARCH BUTTERFLY

Monarchs and viceroys are both poisonous. They have evolved to look alike. Predators remember their bright patterns and stay away.

caterpillars

Caterpillars are baby moths and butterflies. Caterpillars can be smooth and colorful or covered in hair. Some hairy caterpillars can make your skin itch! When it is time to become a pupa, some moth caterpillars build a **COCOON** made from silk. The cocoon is like a pouch that protects the pupa. A butterfly pupa is called a **CHRYSALIS**. Butterflies do not make cocoons.

BANDED WOOLLY - BEAR CATERPILLAR

Insect poop is called frass. Walk in the forest with a parent or guardian at night and listen. Do you hear raindrops, even though the sky is clear? That sound is frass falling from the trees as caterpillars eat!

Butterfly and moth gallery

Skippers are small but mighty butterflies. They can fly very fast and sometimes look like they are skipping across the grass!

SKIPPER BUTTERFLY

SWEETHEART UNDERWING MOTH

CALIFORNIA SISTER BUTTERFLY

PAINTED LICHEN MOTH

ROSY MAPLE MOTH

Brilliant Beetles

More than one-third of all the insects on Earth are beetles. There are almost 390,000 **SPECIES**! Most beetles have two pairs of wings. One pair looks more like a hard shell. These wings are called **ELYTRA**. They protect the wings underneath that a beetle can use for flying. When the elytra are closed, the beetle looks like it has a line down its back.

Beetle antennae can be short and tucked away or long with paddles on them. Some antennae look like a string of beads or a fan.

Baby beetles are called grubs. Many grubs are smooth and light-colored with big abdomens. Grubs often eat roots and other

> **SCIENTIFIC GROUP:** Coleoptera
>
> **SIZE:** Very small to large
>
> **FOOD:** Larvae and adults eat plants, fungus, nectar, and pollen; some adults don't eat
>
> **HOME:** On land; in freshwater and on seashores
>
> **METAMORPHOSIS:** Complete

plant parts. Some have thicker skin like armor and hunt for **PREY**.

NUTTALL'S BLISTER BEETLE

BANDED SEXTON BEETLE

Some beetles rely on more than just their hard shells for defense. Some have chemical weapons. Blister beetles ooze burning oils, and bombardier beetles have explosive farts!

Lovely Ladybugs

Look at this ladybug. Do you see a straight line down its back? That's because it's a beetle! Ladybugs are also called lady beetles. Many lady beetles are red with black spots, but some species are orange, yellow, or even pink. These colors are a warning to **PREDATORS** that the ladybug tastes bad. If a lady beetle is attacked, it can make a stinky fluid ooze from its legs to send its attacker away.

TWO-SPOTTED LADY BEETLE

SCIENTIFIC GROUP: Coleoptera

SIZE: Small

FOOD: Larvae and adults eat small insects; insect eggs, nectar, pollen, and fungus; some eat leaves

HOME: Plants in gardens, fields, meadows, and forests

METAMORPHOSIS: Complete

Lady beetles sleep as adults, too. Many insects find a safe place to sleep for the winter. This safe place may be under tree bark, underneath logs, or even in your home!

Flashy Fireflies

Fireflies are beetles with glowing butts! This glow is called bioluminescence. During the day, fireflies sleep under tree bark or in dry leaves on the ground. At night, male fireflies fly around flashing their lights to attract mates. Female fireflies wait on trees or bushes and flash their lights back if they see a male. Each species of firefly has its own flashing pattern!

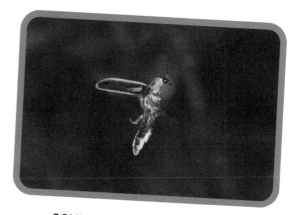

COMMON EASTERN FIREFLY

SCIENTIFIC GROUP: Coleoptera

SIZE: Small

FOOD:
Larvae: Snails, slugs, earthworms, and small bugs
Adults: Pollen, tree sap, and sometimes other fireflies

HOME: Damp, dead leaves and soil, often around streams

METAMORPHOSIS: Complete

Bioluminescent light comes from special chemicals in the firefly's abdomen. When the chemicals mix with oxygen, the firefly's abdomen glows. Fireflies even glow as grubs, sometimes called glowworms.

Some girl fireflies copy the flash pattern of other firefly species. If a boy firefly shows up, it's dinnertime. The girl eats him!

Hard shiny bodies and protective wings keep beetles from drying out. This has helped beetles live almost anywhere on Earth— including deserts and very cold places.

EASTERN FIREFLY

Beetle gallery

DELTA FLOWER SCARAB

ELDERBERRY BORER BEETLE

EASTERN HERCULES BEETLE

EYED CLICK BEETLE

RAINBOW SCARAB BEETLE

Mysterious Mantises

Mantises are built to hunt! They have triangle-shaped heads and big eyes with dark spots. These spots help the bugs focus on prey. Mantis bodies are often green or brown. This helps them blend in with their surroundings so their prey doesn't see them.

Check out the mantis's two front legs. They are folded and covered in spikes. While hunting, a mantis stands very still. When an insect gets close, the mantis quickly grabs it with its spikey legs and eats it.

Mantises lay their eggs in a special case called an ootheca. The ootheca protects the eggs in the cold. Tiny nymphs hatch in spring. They are so hungry that they often eat each other!

CAROLINA MANTIS

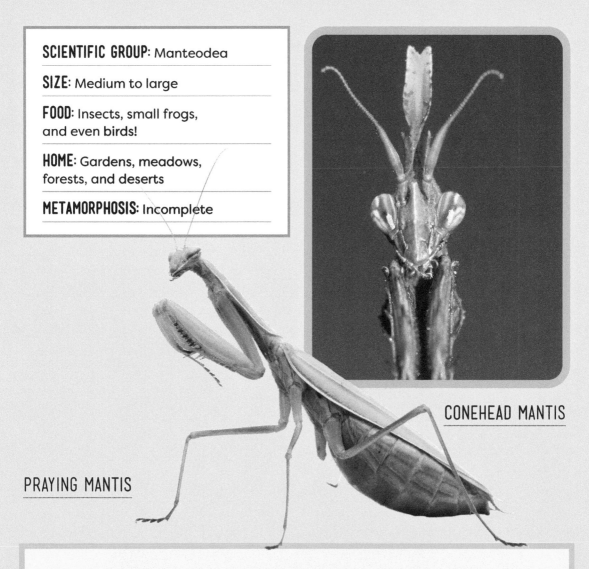

SCIENTIFIC GROUP: Manteodea

SIZE: Medium to large

FOOD: Insects, small frogs, and even birds!

HOME: Gardens, meadows, forests, and deserts

METAMORPHOSIS: Incomplete

CONEHEAD MANTIS

PRAYING MANTIS

When a mantis is scared, it raises its front legs, spreads its wings, and rocks back and forth. This makes it look bigger and meaner!

wondrous wasps

Wasps are flying insects with tiny waists. They have long antennae that might bend like an elbow. Their mouths have mandibles to eat insects. Some wasps have a tongue to lap up nectar.

Girl wasps have long tubes called **OVIPOSITORS** at the end of their abdomens. They use the ovipositor to put their eggs into plants and other insects. Wasps with long ovipositors do not sting.

Some girl wasps have short stingers instead of ovipositors. These wasps sting other bugs and carry them back to the nest to feed to their babies. They also sting other animals to protect their nests. Boy wasps do not have stingers.

ICHNEUMON WASP

Some wasps build nests out of mud or chewed-up plants. Others make their nests in the ground or in the hollows of trees.

SCIENTIFIC GROUP: Hymenoptera

SIZE: Very small to medium

FOOD:
Larvae: Pollen, caterpillars, grubs, and bugs
Adults: Nectar and pollen

HOME: Forests, meadows, deserts, mountains, and gardens

METAMORPHOSIS: Complete

Most stinging wasps are girls. Special girls, called queens, can build nests and lay eggs. The queen's daughters take care of their baby siblings. One special sister will be the next queen.

TARANTULA HAWK WASP

BUSY BEES

Bees have long tongues to lap up nectar from flowers. While they drink, their fuzzy bodies get covered in the flower's pollen. Some bees even have special places on their abdomens and legs to collect pollen. They bring this pollen back to the nest to feed their babies.

AMERICAN BUMBLEBEE

Many bees have very large families to help build the nest and gather food. In the spring, the queen bee begins laying eggs. The adult daughters, called workers, gather pollen and nectar, and take care of their baby sisters.

When the babies become adults in the fall, some special daughters will be queens. Adult sons are called drones. Drones do not gather pollen and they do not sting. Their job is to mate with the queen from another nest.

SCIENTIFIC GROUP: Hymenoptera

SIZE: Small to medium

FOOD: Larvae and adults eat nectar and pollen

HOME: Forests, meadows, deserts, gardens, and fields

METAMORPHOSIS: Complete

EUROPEAN HONEY BEE

CARPENTER BEE

Some bees, like carpenter and digger bees, make very small nests all by themselves. They collect lots of pollen to feed their babies, but do not take care of them.

Honey

Bees are famous for making honey. How do they do it? Well, some bees eat more nectar than they need. They hold this nectar in a special honey stomach. When they return to the hive, these bees throw up the nectar. Other bees eat the nectar again—then *they* throw it back up! After doing this many times, they store the nectar in their nest.

Bees vibrate to warm the hive to 95 degrees Fahrenheit. This evaporates extra water and helps cook the nectar. They flutter their wings to move air around the nectar to keep it from spoiling and to help it cook. Cooking the nectar makes honey. So, honey is cooked bee barf! The bees eat the honey when they cannot find nectar.

EUROPEAN HONEY BEES
MAKING HONEY

Amazing Ants

RED HARVESTER ANT

Worker ants are stinging wasps, but with no wings: They have big jaws to carry things, antennae bent like elbows, and skinny little waists with humps.

The queen ant sets up the nest and lays the eggs. She is larger than other ants because her abdomen is bigger for making eggs. Her daughters are workers. The workers bring back food to the nest to feed the baby ants.

Some daughter workers are soldiers. Soldiers help build the nest, take care of their siblings, and find food. Soldiers have big heads with very strong jaws. They can fight to protect their sisters.

When new queen and drone ants become adults, they have wings to fly away from the nest. The new queen chews off her wings when she lands!

SCIENTIFIC GROUP: Hymenoptera

SIZE: Very small to small

FOOD:
Larvae: Fruits, plants, and small bugs
Adults: Nectar

HOME: Soil, dead leaves, and tree trunks

METAMORPHOSIS: Complete

ANT NEST

Many ants build nests in the ground. These nests have long tunnels and rooms. They look like tiny underground caves! Some ant nests are home to millions of ants.

Some ants are farmers. They cut up leaves to bring back to the nest. Ants use the leaves to grow fungus, which they feed to their babies.

Wasps, bees, and ants gallery

BLACK CARPENTER ANT

STRIPED MINING BEE

LEAFCUTTER ANT

BLUEBERRY BEE

EASTERN CICADA KILLER WASP

great Grasshoppers

Grasshoppers are green and brown to help them blend in with the plants they eat. Their tough front wings protect their large back wings. They use their back wings to fly. Grasshoppers hold their wings like tents over their abdomens. Some have colorful back wings to startle predators when they fly away.

Grasshoppers have large, strong back legs that they use to hop around.

EASTERN LUBBER
GRASSHOPPER NYMPH

Grasshoppers sing to attract mates. They do this by rubbing their back legs against the edge of their hard front wings.

SCIENTIFIC GROUP: Orthoptera

SIZE: Medium to large

FOOD: Herbs and grasses

HOME: Prairies, gardens, meadows, and forests

METAMORPHOSIS: Incomplete

chirping crickets

Crickets have long antennae and also have strong legs for jumping. Their bodies are black, brown, or green. Most crickets have wings that lie flat like a cape. Crickets can't fly very well, and some don't have wings at all!

Crickets come out at night to sing by rubbing their wings together. This is called **STRIDULATING**.

FALL FIELD CRICKET

Some crickets have such beautiful songs, people keep them as pets!

SCIENTIFIC GROUP: Orthoptera

SIZE: Medium

FOOD: Herbs, grasses, plants, and insect eggs

HOME: Prairies, gardens, meadows, and forests

METAMORPHOSIS: Incomplete

Dazzling Dragonflies and Damselflies

Dragonflies and damselflies are fast and graceful predators. They have big compound eyes, short antennae, and large wings. They use their eyes to focus on prey and their legs to snatch insects in the air as they fly. Boys and girls of the same species are often different colors of blue, green, red, and yellow.

Baby dragonflies and damselflies are called **NAIADS** because they hatch and live in water. The naiads eat other bugs that live in the water—including other naiads! When they grow up, the naiads climb out of the water and shed their skins to become adults with wings.

ORANGE BLUET DAMSELFLY

So, what is the difference between a dragonfly and a damselfly? Dragonflies are large with heavy bodies. Their wings are flat, or open, when resting. Damselflies are smaller with thin bodies. They often keep their wings together, or closed, at rest.

When damselflies mate, their bodies form a heart!

BLUE-FACED
MEADOWHAWK DRAGONFLY

SCIENTIFIC GROUP:	Odonata
SIZE:	Medium to large
FOOD:	Other insects
HOME:	Freshwater streams, ponds, and lakes
METAMORPHOSIS:	Incomplete

AMERICAN RUBYSPOT DAMSELFLY

EBONY JEWELWING

ROSEATE SKIMMER

There are about 6,000 different species of dragonflies and damselflies in the world.

Dragonfly and damselfly gallery

TWELVE-SPOTTED SKIMMER

Fantastic Flies

Most insects fly, but only the true flies are called flies! Flies have two wings, small antennae, and big compound eyes that take up most of their faces.

Many flies sip nectar using a proboscis. Others stab prey with their mouth and drink body fluids. Some flies spit onto their food, then absorb it like a sponge. Some flies don't eat at all.

Baby flies are called maggots. They are often smooth and white. Many maggots eat fruit, rotting plants, or dead animals!

GREEN BOTTLE FLY

SCIENTIFIC GROUP: Diptera

SIZE: Very small to medium

FOOD:
Larvae: Plants and animals, fungus, and poop
Adults: Fruit, nectar, pollen, and fungus

HOME: Meadows, forests, swamps, prairies, gardens, and fresh water

METAMORPHOSIS: Complete

*Flies are important **POLLINATORS**! They visit almost as many flowers as bees and other wasps. Many pollinating flies wear the black-and-yellow uniform.*

Mosquito Mania

Mosquitoes are small true flies. There are over 3,700 different species of mosquitoes in the world.

Mosquitoes drink flower nectar. They use their long antennae to smell. They can smell skin, blood, and the air that animals breathe out. This helps them locate a blood meal.

Girl mosquitos use their proboscises to drink blood. The blood helps their eggs develop. Mosquito larvae live in water. They eat algae and sometimes other small insects in the water.

HOUSE MOSQUITO

SCIENTIFIC GROUP: Diptera

SIZE: Small

FOOD:
Larvae: Algae and small bugs
Adult: Boys drink nectar; girls drink nectar and blood

HOME: Ponds, lakes, marshes, swamps, creeks, and still water

METAMORPHOSIS: Complete

Mosquitoes beat their wings more than 500 times per second! This makes their famous whiny buzzing sound.

Glorious Glowworms

Glowworms are the larvae of little flies called predatory fungus gnats. The famous glowworms in New Zealand live in big caves. Blue glowworms live in North America. You can find them in caves, rock cavities, and forests, and along mossy streambanks.

Glowworms spin webs made of silk. They hang on the webs and glow to attract prey. The glowworms eat the creatures that get stuck in their webs.

BLUE FOXFIRE GLOWWORM

SCIENTIFIC GROUP: Diptera

SIZE: Very small

FOOD:
Larvae: Slugs and other small bugs
Adults: Don't eat

HOME: Caves and forests in New Zealand, Australia, and eastern North America

METAMORPHOSIS: Complete

Glowworms may live for a year as larvae, but then live only a few weeks as pupae and adults. Adult boys stop glowing, but adult girls glow bright for the boys to find them.

Fleas: Jumping Experts

Fleas are tiny insects without wings. Fleas live on furry animals like cats and dogs. Their bodies are flat, which helps them move through fur to get to the animals' skin. They bite an animal and drink its blood using their sharp mouthparts. Fleas can bite people, too, and their bites make itchy welts.

Fleas jump using their large back legs. They need to jump far to land on big animals!

CAT FLEA

Fleas can jump more than two feet. For a bug so small, that's like a person jumping over a seven-story building!

SCIENTIFIC GROUP: Siphonaptera

SIZE: Very small

FOOD:
Larvae: Dead bugs
Adults: Blood

HOME: Mammals, birds, and their nests

METAMORPHOSIS: Complete

Elusive Earwigs

Earwigs are flat insects with short, hard front wings that protect their flying wings. They are nocturnal, which means they move around at night. During the day, they hide in cracks and other tight places.

The first things you probably noticed on the earwig are its cerci. They look like big pinchers. Earwigs use their cerci to grab prey, fight off predators, and even to grab girls during mating!

LINED EARWIG

SCIENTIFIC GROUP: Dermaptera

SIZE: Small to medium

FOOD: Plants and insects

HOME: Cool, damp areas like rotting wood; desert species live in rotting cacti

METAMORPHOSIS: Incomplete

Earwigs are devoted mothers. The girls take care of eggs, licking them to keep them clean. They care for the nymphs until they get big enough to take care of themselves.

Wacky Walkingsticks

Walkingsticks look like . . . sticks! They have long bodies and skinny legs that help them blend in on trees and branches. If a bird manages to find and grab one of this bug's skinny legs, a walkingstick can let its leg drop off to escape. When it sheds its skin, the walkingstick may grow a new leg. This bug is so sticklike that many species don't have wings!

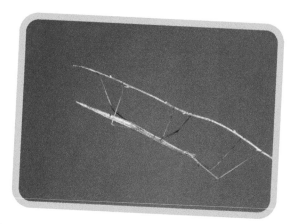

NORTHERN WALKINGSTICK

Walkingstick eggs look like plant seeds. Sometimes birds eat whole walkingsticks and poop out the walkingstick eggs that were inside their meal. The eggs later hatch into little walkingsticks!

SCIENTIFIC GROUP: Phasmida

SIZE: Small to very large

FOOD: Plants, mostly trees

HOME: Forests and meadows

METAMORPHOSIS: Incomplete

Smelly Stink Bugs

Stink bugs are true bugs. All true bugs have mouths like straws. Stink bugs use their mouthparts to stab into their food and suck out the liquid. Their long antennae help them find fruits and other bugs to eat and their wings overlap to make a "V."

Stink bugs stink! They have special places on their abdomen and thorax that make a smelly chemical. The yucky smell keeps predators away.

SPINED SOLDIER BUG

Stink bugs look for shelters to hibernate in over winter. Sometimes they invade people's homes!

SCIENTIFIC GROUP: Hemiptera

SIZE: Small to medium

FOOD: Plants; some eat other insects

HOME: Forests, meadows, gardens, and fields

METAMORPHOSIS: Incomplete

super cicadas

Cicadas are true bugs that can live for a long time. Most of their lives are spent underground, sucking on plant roots in their Eating Stage. Some species live underground for 17 years!

When a cicada nymph is done eating, it crawls aboveground to shed its skin. Sometimes large numbers of cicadas come out all at once. Their skins can cover tree trunks!

Boy cicadas sing for their mates. They use the **TYMBALS** on their abdomens to do this. The tymbal vibrates to make their loud buzzing song.

PERIODICAL CICADA

SCIENTIFIC GROUP: Hemiptera

SIZE: Medium to large

FOOD: Plants

HOME: Forests, meadows, and prairies

METAMORPHOSIS: Incomplete

Cicadas are the loudest insects. Some of their mating songs can be heard from more than a mile away!

spectacular spiders

Spiders are not insects. They are arachnids. Arachnids have eight legs, a big abdomen, and no antennae. Spiders have a **CEPHALOTHORAX** instead of having a head and thorax. On their cephalothorax are their legs, eight eyes, and mouth. Spiders use mouthparts called pedipalps to sense their surroundings.

Spider abdomens have special organs called spinnerets to make silk.

Spiders eat other bugs. Some catch their prey by building a web out of silk. When a bug is caught in its web, the spider quickly injects it with venom. The venom stops the bug from struggling and turns its insides to liquid that the spider can suck up. Spiders don't waste their venom on animals they cannot eat. A spider will bite a person only when it is very scared.

SCIENTIFIC GROUP: Araneae	
SIZE: Small to large	
FOOD: Other bugs	
HOME: Forests, meadows, fields, deserts, prairies, swamps, and streams	
METAMORPHOSIS: None	

PINK CRAB SPIDER

BANDED ARGIOPE SPIDER

BALTIMORE WOLF SPIDER

A baby spider is called a spiderling. Spiderlings can float through the air attached to silk threads. Some spiderlings can drift across entire oceans!

43

Peculiar Pillbugs

Pillbugs have many names: roly-poly, woodlouse, armadillo bug. They are a type of **CRUSTACEAN**—like crabs—with many legs! These little armored creatures live in damp places, such as under rocks and in dead leaves. They have gills and need water to breathe. Most of the time, pillbugs stay in dark places and are active at night.

COMMON EUROPEAN PILLBUG

Pillbugs have a hard exo-skeleton with many sections. They can roll into tiny balls to protect themselves.

SCIENTIFIC GROUP: Isopoda

SIZE: Small

FOOD: Dead plants

HOME: Under rocks and logs in forests, meadows, gardens, and deserts

METAMORPHOSIS: None

More to Discover

Bugs are everywhere! If you keep your eyes and ears open, you can discover a new bug every time to you go outside. Scientists are still discovering new bugs in rain forests and on mountains all around the world.

Scientists who study insects are called entomologists, but many other scientists learn from bugs, too. Bugs help us understand our environment and how diseases are spread. Bugs have even inspired new types of robots!

You can be a scientist, too. There are many people just like you who help entomologists collect more information on bugs. You can be a part of projects that help pollinating bees and flies, migrating monarch butterflies, and many more!

ANT LION

GLOSSARY

ABDOMEN *(AB-duh-muhn):* The "belly" segment of an insect that holds the guts and fat

ARACHNID *(ur-AK-nuhd):* An arthropod with one or two body segments, eight legs, and no antennae

ARTHROPOD *(AAR-thruh-paad):* An animal with an exoskeleton, a body made of segments, and many jointed legs

CEPHALOTHORAX *(seh-fuh-low-THOR-aks):* The body segment of a spider that has its eyes and mouth

CHRYSALIS *(KRI-suh-luhs):* A butterfly pupa

COCOON *(kuh-KOON):* A silk pouch spun by an insect larva to protect the pupa

COMPOUND EYES *(COM-pownd IZE):* Eyes that are made up of hundreds of little lenses that are best at seeing movement

CRUSTACEAN *(kruh-STAY-shun):* An arthropod that has two pairs of antennae, jointed legs, and a hard exoskeleton

ELYTRA *(el-EYE-truh):* The hard front wings of a beetle

EVOLVE *(ee-VAALV):* When a species has changes in its body or behaviors over time

EXOSKELETON *(ek-sew-SKEH-luh-tn):* Hard skin that must be shed as the animal grows

INSECT *(IN-sekt):* An arthropod that has three body segments, six legs, and two antennae

LARVA/LARVAE *(LAAR-vuh/LAAR-vee):* An insect in the Eating Stage of complete metamorphosis

METAMORPHOSIS *(meh-tuh-MOR-fuh-suhs):* The stages an insect goes through as it grows and changes

NAIAD *(NYE-ad):* A damselfly or dragon-fly in the Eating Stage

NYMPH *(NIMF):* An insect in the Eating Stage of incomplete metamorphosis

OCELLI *(uh-CHEH-lee):* Simple eyes used to sense light

OVIPOSITOR *(oh-vuh-PAA-zuh-ter):* The tube on a female insect's abdomen that is used to lay eggs

POLLINATOR *(PAWL-in-a-ter):* An animal that brings pollen from one flower to another

PREDATOR *(PREH-duh-ter):* An animal that hunts and eats other animals

PREY *(PRAY):* An animal that is eaten by another animal

PROBOSCIS *(proh-BAA-skuhs):* A long insect mouth that is like a drinking straw

PUPA/PUPAE *(PYOO-puh/PYOO-pee):* An insect that is changing from larva to adult in the Sleeping Stage of complete metamorphosis

SPECIES *(SPEE-sheez):* A group of living things that have many things in common and can produce others of their kind

SPIRACLES *(SPEE-ruh-klz):* The openings on an insect's side that allow it to breathe

STRIDULATION *(strih-dyu-LAY-shun):* When an insect makes a sound by rubbing one body part against another

THORAX *(THOR-aks):* The "chest" segment of an insect where its legs and wings are attached

TYMBAL *(TIM-ball):* A special organ on a cicada's abdomen (and some moths) that makes sound

ABOUT THE AUTHOR

REA MANDERINO, PhD spent her childhood raising tiger swallowtails on the parsley in her grandmother's garden. Her passion for insects ignited with her high school insect collection. She went on to receive her PhD in entomology from the State University of New York College of Environmental Science and Forestry.